Climates

RUTH FAINLIGHT

to Hal
with warm regard
from Ruth.

April 3rd 1985

BLOODAXE BOOKS

ISBN: 0 906427 34 7

First published 1983 by
Bloodaxe Books Ltd,
P.O. Box 1SN,
Newcastle upon Tyne NE99 1SN.

Second impression 1984.

Bloodaxe Books Ltd acknowledges
the financial assistance of Northern Arts.

Printed in Great Britain by
Tyneside Free Press Workshop Ltd, Newcastle upon Tyne.

Further...Closer

First day of the second half of another year.
Again the evenings will be shorter, mornings later,
the centre of the solar system further away.

This fear of being exiled further from the source,
trapped in the desolation of my own centre,
where frozen winter will be autumn's only harvest.

What could be further than my soul from any centre
of light and warmth and energy? If the sun is a jewel
in its creator's crown, his face is turned away.

But what horror, if he should swerve round and fix his gaze
on me. Nothing I was or thought could endure those eyes
as they came closer, and cauterized my darkest centre.

And yet, I still keep moving closer to the furnace-
centre, that jewelled horror now as cool as water,
where he reigns, lord of all knowledge, where night and day

have the same length, winter and summer eternally stopped
at Heaven's equinoctial centre, closer towards
the promised revelation of his other face.

While Summer Runs Its Course

Somewhere a few miles south or north
the sun is shining. Or closer still,
straight up, above the cloud, a brilliant
azure summer sky, unlike
this pallid swathing round the grey
church tower, asserts the actual season.
But here, a milky hush obscures
the day, and birds behave as though
it's almost twilight, not late morning.

Today this muffled noon conforms
well with my mood—it seems to promise
change (the birdsong strengthens, blueness
curdles, shadows harden) yet
everything remains potential.
Later, if the local pattern
holds, the sky will clear and colours
throb and deepen into glory
just before the sunset chorus.

Or the day might end in storm,
piling clouds above the trees
that form a curtain closing in
the garden, and the birds go silent –
which would answer to another
aspect of my need: a sudden
rain to filter through the rocks
and roots and graves, be purified
into the universal water.

This year, while summer runs its course
and I attempt the furthest zones –
expose myself once more to all
those different climates of the past –
I expect to alter as often
as the weather. And if again
the sun and rain produce their normal
miracle, the harvest, perhaps
I too will come to that reward.

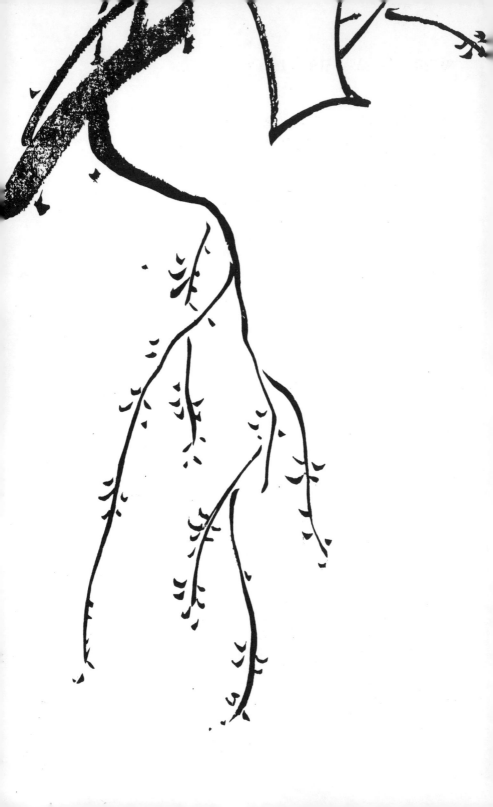

The Distant View

Summer rain
streaming down the windowpane
is the sound of the wind,
and shaking trees,
heavy with their fullest leaves,
are the shape of the wind.

Ten years looking at the same scene,
the same tower, the same steeple.
Either the church is slowly sinking,
or the trees are growing taller.

Always the birdsong. The first
sound at dawn: pigeons
in the chimney, with the changeless message
of another morning.
And only the heaviest rainstorm
can drown for a moment
their mechanical calling.

Flaunting its burden of foliage
every branch and twig moves
in a different direction: thousands
of despairing gestures—an outdated style.
Inside the house, the silence,
except for wind, rain, birds,
makes such extravagant
expressiveness even less viable.

Then, between showers, the flat grey sky
is stretched apart, coagulates
to cloud. The horizon returns. The trees
are calmer. Soon the sun will be setting.
Birds begin to celebrate
that blue and crimson certainty.
Everything looks smaller, clearer,
further away, and quickly, before
I lose the distant view and rain
comes down again I close the curtains.

Like shadows on the lawn –

sentences form in my head,
float in and out of my mind.
The thinner the cloud and stronger
the source of light, the firmer
the outline: a tentative smile
spreading across an unknown
face. The pale sky moves
above the empty garden,
and moods and memories
as seeming-motiveless
as this uncertain weather
follow each other, colour
my thoughts, then fade before
expressed by tears or words
or action. But that stranger,
with features so familiar
I might be looking in
a mirror, could determine
my future if I will
accept what she bestows,
and every shadow harden
wane and disappear
when noonday sunlight burns
away the morning haze.

Another Variation

Motor mowers, shrieking children,
and the slamming of car doors.
Sunday dinner smells. Summer
in the village. Soon the bells
will start. A stranger still, tonight
I shan't go to the pub, but stay
here in my room. Then, the only
sound, after everyone
has gone back home and dogs have stopped
their barking, will be my own pen scratching,
matches striking, papers torn
perhaps as I reject another
variation of this poem.

Angel from the North

Now, between July and autumn,
August makes its own season.
The clouds seem higher, piled in sharper
whites and darker greys, the sky
already colder—arctic tones
above the glowing apple trees,
laden with a better crop
than these ten years I've lived here. Next month
such rain would strip the leaves, every
morning raise another ring
of tawny mushrooms, mournful flocks
of martins gathering for their
long journey south. Today, the lawn
shows only greener and more livid
when the storm stops, and still the sun
strikes hot before a further bank
of cloud blots out the light, moving
like an angel from the north –
whose fiery sword of frost will bring
the apples down to rot among
the sodden leaves and faded grass,
and mark the garden like the first-born.

Vanguards

Autumn begins with drizzle and the smell
of burning stubble. Though I shut all windows,
acrid smoke permeates the house.

That sound is not artillery nor rain,
but straw's dry crackle. Only from the attic
am I high enough above the garden trees

to see those black paths streaked across pale fields
where ash becomes the final harvest
and birds rise in alarm. Later, at twilight,

the distant glow, orange and red, with its nimbus
of white, could be a battle-ground,
and every separate fire a gutted tank –

vanguards threatening a long campaign
of skirmishes as winter closes in
to gain its yearly total victory.

An Unmarked Ship

An unmarked ship, entering
the harbour of an undefended
town: autumn bears down on the land.
Driven by a north-west wind,
banks of cloud are the weight of sail
carried on its towering masts,

and that relentless grinding back
and forth of harvesting machines
across the fields becomes the distant
shouts for help and last attempts
of the inhabitants to save
themselves before the plundering starts.

Red Sky at Night . . . .

Clouds in horizontal bars
lit gold beneath, shaded mauve
above, with flame and scarlet centres.

Puce and dove become a pure
blue sky that deepens, heightens. Red
brick house, red roof-tiles, rose-hips

and crimson autumn leaves. And all of it
my delight, though I am more
one of the hungry flock than a shepherd.

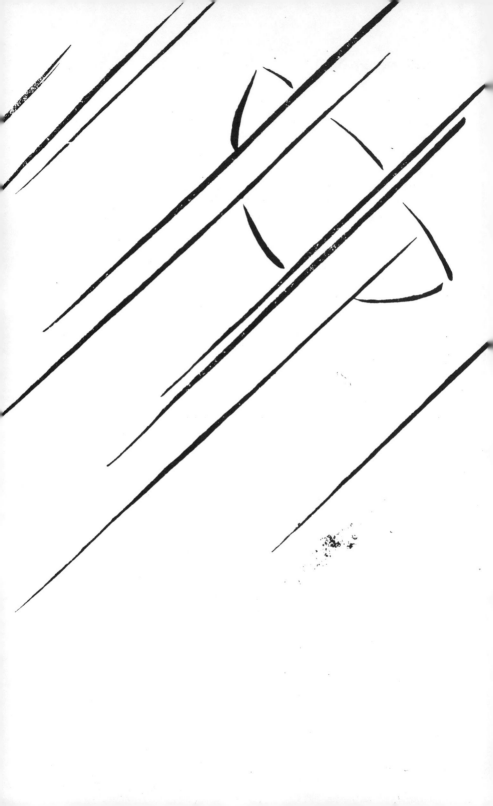

Anticipated

This month I've watched the moon through every change
from thinnest crescent into ripeness, from August
langour into clear September. Unseen
between two darknesses, full moon will be
tomorrow morning, just before noon. Tomorrow
night, hours after the unmarked climax,
her strength already waning, will be too late.
Tonight her energies are at their height.

Full moon used to awe me, craze me—now
I feel equal to her power. This
moment perhaps I too have reached an acme,
and the over-arching sky, the garden trees
with their rustlings and shadows, their nightingale-language,
are satellites circling around the centre
everything on earth anticipates
and this one night allows me to become.

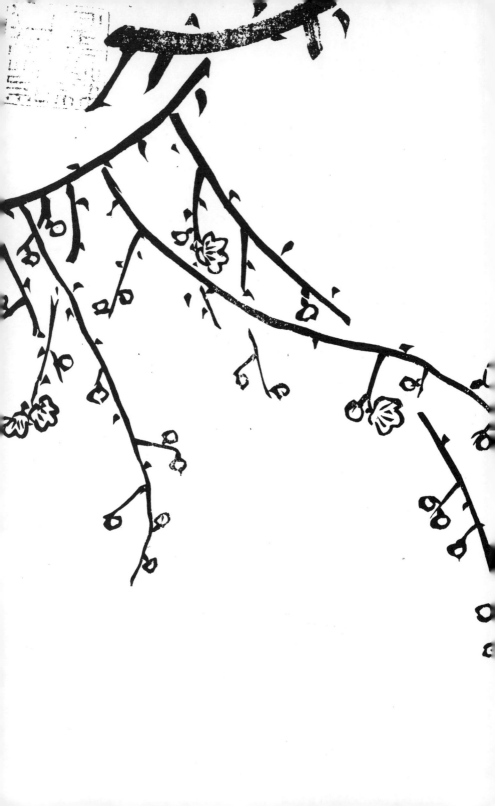

To Break this Silence

Wind and trees and birds, this vague and always
changing weather: how they cut me off
from him with whom I share my house and life,
and I am altered by the seasons' power.

Hours each day together. Yet not enough
to counterweigh the glamour I succumb to,
those hours spent staring at the fire. It seems
that nothing happens but the rain and sunset,

night-mist curling through the hedges. The habit
of our mutual isolation forces me
to seek the most persuasive words to break
this silence: the key and explanation why

the radiance of a sphere of light against
the clouded autumn sky, swathing the moon
like fruit around its stone, confirms that we
have come to be the other's space and climate.

Ruth Fainlight has published eight books of poems, including *Cages* (1966) and *To See the Matter Clearly* (1968) from Macmillan, and *The Region's Violence* (1973), *Another Full Moon* (1976), *Sibyls And Others* (1980), and *Fifteen to Infinity* (1983) from Hutchinson. Her translation from the Portuguese of a selection of poems by Sophia de Mello Breyner is forthcoming from Carcanet.

Ruth Fainlight's mother was born in what was then a small town on the eastern borders of the Austro-Hungarian Empire and is now part of the Soviet Union, while her father was born in London, and she herself in New York City. She has been an expatriate for 35 years but still retains her American citizenship.

The prints in *Climates* are by **Ki Batei** (1734-1810), one of the Japanese scholar-painters of the 'literati' movement. These artists stressed the kinship between painting, calligraphy and poetry in the form of *haiga*—the kind of drawing that was half decoration and half illustration of the verse. Ki Batei's master was Yosa Buson, the 'second Pillar of Haiku' after Basho, and one of Japan's greatest artists.